WHO WAS THE
HAIR-CARE
MILLIONAIRE?

MADAM
C. J. WALKER

Mary Kay

Carson

Enslow Elementary

an imprint of

Enslow Publishers, Inc.

 40 Industrial Road
Box 398
Berkeley Heights, NJ 07922
USA

http://www.enslow.com

S0-BSN-532

CONTENTS

WORDS TO KNOW

charities—Groups that help the poor and needy.

millionaire—Someone who is worth a million or more dollars.

orphan—A child with no parents.

plantation—A large farm with slaves or workers.

scalp—The skin under the hair on the head.

R0429131474

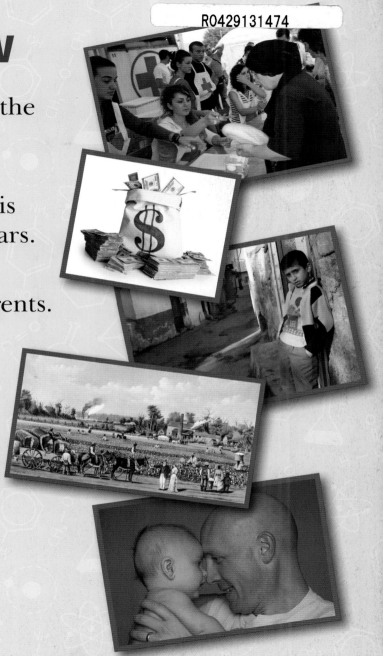

Many people worked on a cotton plantation.

RAGS TO RICHES

Madam C. J. Walker was born on a **plantation**. Her parents had been slaves. Walker lived years ago, before women could vote. At that time being African American made everything harder. But she started a business. She became a **millionaire**. How did she do it?

Madam C. J. Walker

TOUGH
START

Walker started working in the cotton fields when she was five years old. There was little time for school. She became an **orphan** two years later. Both her parents died. She needed money to live. So, she washed clothes for money. Walker was young when she got married. She had a baby when she was seventeen.

In 1867, Walker was born in this cabin. The cabin was on a Louisiana plantation.

WESTLAKE
LAUNDRY.

HARD LIFE

Walker's husband died a few years later. She moved to St. Louis, Missouri, and worked washing clothes.

Walker usually wore a scarf. Her hair was falling out. Her **scalp** was unhealthy. She tried different hair products. Nothing helped.

DREAM
ANSWER

Walker decided to make her own hair product.
What would help hair grow? She prayed for an
answer. Walker had a dream.
In it, a man told her the
ingredients. She tried mixing
the ingredients and using
them on her head. Her hair
grew back!

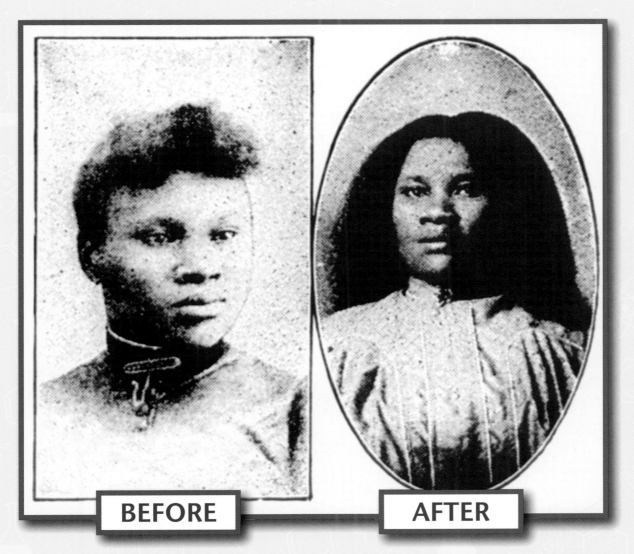

BEFORE

AFTER

These photos show Walker before and after using her "Wonderful Hair Grower."

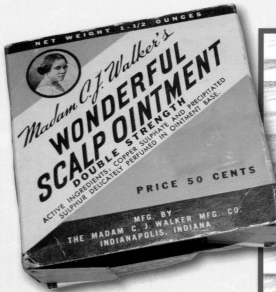

Madam C. J. Walker invented a whole line of beauty products for African-American women.

Walker began selling hair-care products door to door.

GROWING
BUSINESS

Walker called her new product "Wonderful Hair Grower." She sold it by knocking on doors. She went from house to house. Many women bought her products and shampoos. Walker's business grew fast.

Walker showed women how to use her products.

13

HAIR-CARE
COMPANY

A Real Opportunity for Women who wish to become Independent.

Mme. WALKER'S SYSTEM

of Scientific Scalp Treatment and Sales of her Hair Preparations are giving support to more than 100,000 people in this Industry. Come in and learn how.

Madam C.J. Walker's hair-care company was successful. Lots of people worked for her. Walker opened beauty shops. She taught women how to sell. She sold her products in other countries, too.

Madam C. J. Walker helped many African-American women. She gave them a new place to work.

SHARE THE
WEALTH

Walker became rich. She lived in a mansion. Walker gave a lot of money to schools and **charities**. She had been poor and an orphan. Walker wanted to help others. She changed their lives, too.

Walker's home on the Hudson River in New York was named Villa Lewaro.

MODEL
MILLIONAIRE

Walker also changed people's minds. Some people did not think she could become rich. But she became the first African-American woman millionaire. She did it with hard work. She never gave up. Her example helped others follow their dreams, too.

Madam C. J. Walker, photographed with Booker T. Washington (man holding his hat) and other African-American leaders.

ACTIVITY: HOMEMADE
BUBBLE BATH

DO NOT DO THIS ACTIVITY IF YOU ARE ALLERGIC TO FOOD COLORING, PERFUME, OR SCENTED OILS.

You Will Need:

- Clear fragrance-free shampoo, 1/2 cup
- Water, 3/4 cup
- Salt, 1/2 teaspoon
- Bowl
- Spoon
- Empty jar or bottle with lid
- Food coloring (optional)
- Perfume or scented oil (optional)
- Self-adhesive label (or paper and tape)
- Pen or pencil

What To Do:

1. Pour water and shampoo into a bowl. Stir gently.

2. Add salt, stir, and wait for mixture to thicken.

3. Stir in food coloring if you want the bubble bath to be colored, and a drop of perfume or scented oil if you want a fragrance.

4. Pour your new bubble bath into a jar or bottle.

5. Make a label for your product. What will you name it?

LEARN MORE

BOOKS

Hobkirk, Lori. *Madam C. J. Walker.* Mankato, Minn.: Child's World, 2009.

Krohn, Katherine. *Madam C. J. Walker and New Cosmetics.* Mankato, Minn.: Capstone Press, 2007.

Lasky, Kathryn. *Vision of Beauty: The Story of Sarah Breedlove Walker.* Cambridge, Mass.: Candlewick Press, 2003.

WEB SITES

Madam C.J. Walker: The Official Web Site

<http://www.madamcjwalker.com/students-teachers/>

Inventor of the Week: Madame C. J. Walker

<http://web.mit.edu/invent/iow/cjwalker.html>

INDEX

Enslow Elementary, an imprint of Enslow Publishers, Inc.

Enslow Elementary® is a registered trademark of Enslow Publishers, Inc.

Copyright © 2012 by Mary Kay Carson

All rights reserved.

No part of this book may be reproduced by any means without the written permission of the publisher.

Library of Congress Cataloging-in-Publication Data

Carson, Mary Kay.

  Who was the hair-care millionaire? Madame C.J. Walker / Mary Kay Carson.

    p. cm. — (I like inventors!)

  Includes index.

  ISBN 978-0-7660-3973-5

  1. Walker, C. J., Madam, 1867–1919—Juvenile literature. 2. African American women executives—Biography—Juvenile literature. 3. Cosmetics industry—United States—History—Juvenile literature. 4. Women millionaires—United States—Biography—Juvenile literature. I. Title.

  HD9970.5.C672W3536 2012

  338.7′66855—dc23

  [B]

                                          2011029277

Future editions:

Paperback ISBN 978-1-4644-0133-6

ePUB ISBN 978-1-4645-1040-3

PDF ISBN 978-1-4645-1040-0

Printed in China

012012 Leo Paper Group, Heshan City, Guangdong, China

10 9 8 7 6 5 4 3 2 1

To Our Readers: We have done our best to make sure all Internet Addresses in this book were active and appropriate when we went to press. However, the author and the publisher have no control over and assume no liability for the material available on those Internet sites or on other Web sites they may link to. Any comments or suggestions can be sent by e-mail to comments@enslow.com or to the address on the back cover.

Series Consultant:
Duncan R. Jamieson, PhD
Professor of History
Ashland University
Ashland, OH

Series Literacy Consultant:
Allan A. De Fina, PhD
Dean, College of Education/Professor of Literacy Education
New Jersey City University
Past President of the New Jersey Reading Association

Photo Credits: © 1999 Artville, LLC, p. 9; Courtesy of the Indiana Historical Society, pp. 5, 7, 23; Daniel Hurst/Photos.com, p. 3 (millionaire), 22; Enslow Publishers, Inc., p. 12 (right); kojoku/Shutterstock.com, p. 3 (charities); Library of Congress, Prints and Photographs pp. 3 (plantation), 4; Madam C. J. Walker Collection, Courtesy of the Indiana Historical Society, pp. 11, 13, 14, 15, 19; National Park Service, p. 16; Photograph Collection, Archives and Special Collections Department, Frazar Memorial Library, McNeese State University, p. 8; Property of Black Legacy Images; Dawn Spears, President, pp. 1 (tin), 2, 10, 12 (box); Shutterstock.com, pp. 1 (woman), 3 (orphan, scalp), 20, 21.

Cover Photo: Shutterstock.com; Courtesy of the Indiana Historical Society (inset).